Date:_____

What Am I grateful for?

_____
_____
_____
_____
_____
_____

What is my intention for the day?

_____
_____
_____
_____
_____
_____

What are my affirmations for the day?

_____
_____
_____
_____
_____
_____

An experience I transformed to serve me through a change in perception
___
___
___
___
___
___
___

Daily Reflections

___
___
___
___
___
___
___
___
___
___
___
___
___
___
___

Date:_____

What Am I grateful for?

_____
_____
_____
_____
_____
_____

What is my intention for the day?

_____
_____
_____
_____
_____
_____

What are my affirmations for the day?

_____
_____
_____
_____
_____
_____
_____

An experience I transformed to serve me through a change in perception

_____
_____
_____
_____
_____
_____

Daily Reflections

_____
_____
_____
_____
_____
_____
_____
_____
_____
_____
_____
_____
_____
_____
_____

Date:_____

What Am I grateful for?
_____
_____
_____
_____
_____
_____
_____

What is my intention for the day?
_____
_____
_____
_____
_____
_____
_____

What are my affirmations for the day?
_____
_____
_____
_____
_____
_____
_____

An experience I transformed to serve me through a change in perception
_____
_____
_____
_____
_____
_____
_____

Daily Reflections

_____
_____
_____
_____
_____
_____
_____
_____
_____
_____
_____
_____
_____
_____
_____
_____

Date:_____

What Am I grateful for?

_____
_____
_____
_____
_____
_____

What is my intention for the day?

_____
_____
_____
_____
_____
_____

What are my affirmations for the day?

_____
_____
_____
_____
_____
_____
_____

An experience I transformed to serve me through a change in perception

Daily Reflections

Date:_____

What Am I grateful for?
_____
_____
_____
_____
_____
_____

What is my intention for the day?
_____
_____
_____
_____
_____
_____

What are my affirmations for the day?
_____
_____
_____
_____
_____
_____

An experience I transformed to serve me through a change in perception

_____
_____
_____
_____
_____
_____

Daily Reflections

_____
_____
_____
_____
_____
_____
_____
_____
_____
_____
_____
_____
_____
_____

Date:_____

What Am I grateful for?

_____
_____
_____
_____
_____
_____
_____

What is my intention for the day?

_____
_____
_____
_____
_____
_____
_____

What are my affirmations for the day?

_____
_____
_____
_____
_____
_____
_____

An experience I transformed to serve me through a change in perception

___

Daily Reflections

___

Date:_____

What Am I grateful for?

_____
_____
_____
_____
_____
_____

What is my intention for the day?

_____
_____
_____
_____
_____
_____

What are my affirmations for the day?

_____
_____
_____
_____
_____
_____
_____

An experience I transformed to serve me through a change in perception
_____
_____
_____
_____
_____
_____
_____

Daily Reflections

_____
_____
_____
_____
_____
_____
_____
_____
_____
_____
_____
_____
_____
_____

Date:_____

What Am I grateful for?

_____
_____
_____
_____
_____
_____

What is my intention for the day?

_____
_____
_____
_____
_____
_____

What are my affirmations for the day?

_____
_____
_____
_____
_____
_____

An experience I transformed to serve me through a change in perception

Daily Reflections

Date:_____

What Am I grateful for?

_____
_____
_____
_____
_____

What is my intention for the day?

_____
_____
_____
_____
_____

What are my affirmations for the day?

_____
_____
_____
_____
_____
_____

An experience I transformed to serve me through a change in perception
___

Daily Reflections
___

Date:_____

What Am I grateful for?

_____
_____
_____
_____
_____
_____
_____

What is my intention for the day?

_____
_____
_____
_____
_____
_____
_____

What are my affirmations for the day?

_____
_____
_____
_____
_____
_____
_____

An experience I transformed to serve me through a change in perception
_____
_____
_____
_____
_____
_____
_____

Daily Reflections
_____
_____
_____
_____
_____
_____
_____
_____
_____
_____
_____
_____
_____
_____
_____

Date:_____

What Am I grateful for?
_____
_____
_____
_____
_____
_____

What is my intention for the day?
_____
_____
_____
_____
_____
_____

What are my affirmations for the day?
_____
_____
_____
_____
_____
_____
_____

An experience I transformed to serve me through a change in perception

Daily Reflections

Date:_____

What Am I grateful for?
_____
_____
_____
_____
_____

What is my intention for the day?
_____
_____
_____
_____
_____

What are my affirmations for the day?
_____
_____
_____
_____
_____
_____

An experience I transformed to serve me through a change in perception

Daily Reflections

Date:_____

What Am I grateful for?

_____
_____
_____
_____
_____
_____
_____

What is my intention for the day?

_____
_____
_____
_____
_____
_____
_____

What are my affirmations for the day?

_____
_____
_____
_____
_____
_____
_____

An experience I transformed to serve me through a change in perception
___

___

___

___

___

___

___

Daily Reflections

___

___

___

___

___

___

___

___

___

___

___

___

___

___

___

Date:_____

What Am I grateful for?
_____
_____
_____
_____
_____
_____
_____

What is my intention for the day?
_____
_____
_____
_____
_____
_____
_____

What are my affirmations for the day?
_____
_____
_____
_____
_____
_____
_____

An experience I transformed to serve me through a change in perception

Daily Reflections

Date:_____

What Am I grateful for?
_____
_____
_____
_____
_____
_____
_____

What is my intention for the day?
_____
_____
_____
_____
_____
_____
_____

What are my affirmations for the day?
_____
_____
_____
_____
_____
_____
_____

An experience I transformed to serve me through a change in perception

Daily Reflections

Date:_____

What Am I grateful for?

_____
_____
_____
_____
_____
_____

What is my intention for the day?

_____
_____
_____
_____
_____
_____

What are my affirmations for the day?

_____
_____
_____
_____
_____
_____
_____

An experience I transformed to serve me through a change in perception

Daily Reflections

Date:_____

What Am I grateful for?

_____
_____
_____
_____
_____
_____

What is my intention for the day?

_____
_____
_____
_____
_____
_____

What are my affirmations for the day?

_____
_____
_____
_____
_____
_____

An experience I transformed to serve me through a change in perception

___

Daily Reflections

___

Date:_____

What Am I grateful for?

_____
_____
_____
_____
_____
_____

What is my intention for the day?

_____
_____
_____
_____
_____
_____

What are my affirmations for the day?

_____
_____
_____
_____
_____
_____

An experience I transformed to serve me through a change in perception
_____
_____
_____
_____
_____
_____
_____

Daily Reflections

_____
_____
_____
_____
_____
_____
_____
_____
_____
_____
_____
_____
_____
_____

Date:_____

What Am I grateful for?

_____
_____
_____
_____
_____
_____

What is my intention for the day?

_____
_____
_____
_____
_____
_____

What are my affirmations for the day?

_____
_____
_____
_____
_____
_____
_____

An experience I transformed to serve me through a change in perception
_____
_____
_____
_____
_____
_____
_____

Daily Reflections

_____
_____
_____
_____
_____
_____
_____
_____
_____
_____
_____
_____
_____
_____
_____

Date:_____

What Am I grateful for?

_____
_____
_____
_____
_____
_____

What is my intention for the day?

_____
_____
_____
_____
_____
_____

What are my affirmations for the day?

_____
_____
_____
_____
_____
_____
_____

An experience I transformed to serve me through a change in perception

Daily Reflections

Date:_____

What Am I grateful for?
___
___
___
___
___
___

What is my intention for the day?
___
___
___
___
___
___

What are my affirmations for the day?
___
___
___
___
___
___
___

An experience I transformed to serve me through a change in perception

Daily Reflections

Date:_____

What Am I grateful for?
_____
_____
_____
_____
_____
_____

What is my intention for the day?
_____
_____
_____
_____
_____
_____

What are my affirmations for the day?
_____
_____
_____
_____
_____
_____
_____

An experience I transformed to serve me through a change in perception
___

Daily Reflections
___

Date:_____

What Am I grateful for?

_____
_____
_____
_____
_____
_____

What is my intention for the day?

_____
_____
_____
_____
_____
_____

What are my affirmations for the day?

_____
_____
_____
_____
_____
_____
_____

An experience I transformed to serve me through a change in perception
___

Daily Reflections

Date:_____

What Am I grateful for?
_____
_____
_____
_____
_____
_____

What is my intention for the day?
_____
_____
_____
_____
_____
_____

What are my affirmations for the day?
_____
_____
_____
_____
_____
_____
_____

An experience I transformed to serve me through a change in perception

Daily Reflections

Date:_____

What Am I grateful for?

_____
_____
_____
_____
_____
_____

What is my intention for the day?

_____
_____
_____
_____
_____
_____

What are my affirmations for the day?

_____
_____
_____
_____
_____
_____
_____

An experience I transformed to serve me through a change in perception
___

Daily Reflections

Date:_____

What Am I grateful for?

_____
_____
_____
_____
_____
_____

What is my intention for the day?

_____
_____
_____
_____
_____
_____

What are my affirmations for the day?

_____
_____
_____
_____
_____
_____

An experience I transformed to serve me through a change in perception
___
___
___
___
___
___
___

Daily Reflections
___
___
___
___
___
___
___
___
___
___
___
___
___
___
___
___
___

Date:_____

What Am I grateful for?

_____
_____
_____
_____
_____
_____

What is my intention for the day?

_____
_____
_____
_____
_____
_____

What are my affirmations for the day?

_____
_____
_____
_____
_____
_____

An experience I transformed to serve me through a change in perception
___

Daily Reflections

___

Date:_____

What Am I grateful for?

_____
_____
_____
_____
_____
_____

What is my intention for the day?

_____
_____
_____
_____
_____
_____

What are my affirmations for the day?

_____
_____
_____
_____
_____
_____

An experience I transformed to serve me through a change in perception

___

Daily Reflections

___

Date:_____

What Am I grateful for?

_____
_____
_____
_____
_____
_____

What is my intention for the day?

_____
_____
_____
_____
_____
_____

What are my affirmations for the day?

_____
_____
_____
_____
_____
_____
_____

An experience I transformed to serve me through a change in perception
___

___

___

___

___

___

___

Daily Reflections

___

___

___

___

___

___

___

___

___

___

___

___

___

___

___

Date:_____

What Am I grateful for?

_____
_____
_____
_____
_____
_____

What is my intention for the day?

_____
_____
_____
_____
_____
_____

What are my affirmations for the day?

_____
_____
_____
_____
_____
_____
_____

An experience I transformed to serve me through a change in perception

Daily Reflections

Date:_____

What Am I grateful for?
_____
_____
_____
_____
_____
_____

What is my intention for the day?
_____
_____
_____
_____
_____
_____

What are my affirmations for the day?
_____
_____
_____
_____
_____
_____
_____

An experience I transformed to serve me through a change in perception
_____
_____
_____
_____
_____
_____

Daily Reflections

_____
_____
_____
_____
_____
_____
_____
_____
_____
_____
_____
_____
_____
_____
_____

Date:_____

What Am I grateful for?
_____
_____
_____
_____
_____
_____

What is my intention for the day?
_____
_____
_____
_____
_____
_____

What are my affirmations for the day?
_____
_____
_____
_____
_____
_____
_____
_____

An experience I transformed to serve me through a change in perception

Daily Reflections

Date:_____

What Am I grateful for?

_____
_____
_____
_____
_____
_____

What is my intention for the day?

_____
_____
_____
_____
_____
_____

What are my affirmations for the day?

_____
_____
_____
_____
_____
_____
_____

An experience I transformed to serve me through a change in perception
___

Daily Reflections
___

Date:_____

What Am I grateful for?

_____
_____
_____
_____
_____
_____

What is my intention for the day?

_____
_____
_____
_____
_____
_____

What are my affirmations for the day?

_____
_____
_____
_____
_____
_____
_____

An experience I transformed to serve me through a change in perception

___

Daily Reflections

___

Date:_____

What Am I grateful for?

_____
_____
_____
_____
_____
_____

What is my intention for the day?

_____
_____
_____
_____
_____
_____

What are my affirmations for the day?

_____
_____
_____
_____
_____
_____
_____

An experience I transformed to serve me through a change in perception

Daily Reflections

Date:_____

What Am I grateful for?

_____
_____
_____
_____
_____
_____

What is my intention for the day?

_____
_____
_____
_____
_____
_____

What are my affirmations for the day?

_____
_____
_____
_____
_____
_____
_____
_____

An experience I transformed to serve me through a change in perception
_____
_____
_____
_____
_____
_____
_____

Daily Reflections
_____
_____
_____
_____
_____
_____
_____
_____
_____
_____
_____
_____
_____
_____

Date:_____

What Am I grateful for?

_____
_____
_____
_____
_____
_____
_____

What is my intention for the day?

_____
_____
_____
_____
_____
_____
_____

What are my affirmations for the day?

_____
_____
_____
_____
_____
_____
_____
_____

An experience I transformed to serve me through a change in perception

Daily Reflections

Date:_____

What Am I grateful for?

_____
_____
_____
_____
_____
_____

What is my intention for the day?

_____
_____
_____
_____
_____
_____

What are my affirmations for the day?

_____
_____
_____
_____
_____
_____
_____

An experience I transformed to serve me through a change in perception

___

___

___

___

___

Daily Reflections

___

___

___

___

___

___

___

___

___

___

___

___

___

___

___

Date:_____

What Am I grateful for?

_____
_____
_____
_____
_____
_____

What is my intention for the day?

_____
_____
_____
_____
_____
_____

What are my affirmations for the day?

_____
_____
_____
_____
_____
_____
_____

An experience I transformed to serve me through a change in perception

Daily Reflections

Date:_____

What Am I grateful for?

_____
_____
_____
_____
_____
_____

What is my intention for the day?

_____
_____
_____
_____
_____
_____

What are my affirmations for the day?

_____
_____
_____
_____
_____
_____
_____

An experience I transformed to serve me through a change in perception
_____
_____
_____
_____
_____
_____
_____

Daily Reflections
_____
_____
_____
_____
_____
_____
_____
_____
_____
_____
_____
_____
_____
_____

Date:_____

What Am I grateful for?
_____
_____
_____
_____
_____
_____

What is my intention for the day?
_____
_____
_____
_____
_____
_____

What are my affirmations for the day?
_____
_____
_____
_____
_____
_____
_____

An experience I transformed to serve me through a change in perception

_____
_____
_____
_____
_____
_____
_____

Daily Reflections

_____
_____
_____
_____
_____
_____
_____
_____
_____
_____
_____
_____
_____
_____
_____

Date:_____

What Am I grateful for?

_____
_____
_____
_____
_____
_____

What is my intention for the day?

_____
_____
_____
_____
_____
_____

What are my affirmations for the day?

_____
_____
_____
_____
_____
_____
_____

An experience I transformed to serve me through a change in perception

Daily Reflections

Date:_____

What Am I grateful for?

_____
_____
_____
_____
_____
_____

What is my intention for the day?

_____
_____
_____
_____
_____
_____

What are my affirmations for the day?

_____
_____
_____
_____
_____
_____
_____

An experience I transformed to serve me through a change in perception
_____
_____
_____
_____
_____
_____

Daily Reflections
_____
_____
_____
_____
_____
_____
_____
_____
_____
_____
_____
_____
_____

Date:_____

What Am I grateful for?

_____
_____
_____
_____
_____
_____

What is my intention for the day?

_____
_____
_____
_____
_____
_____

What are my affirmations for the day?

_____
_____
_____
_____
_____
_____
_____

An experience I transformed to serve me through a change in perception
___
___
___
___
___
___
___

Daily Reflections

___
___
___
___
___
___
___
___
___
___
___
___
___
___
___
___

Date:_____

What Am I grateful for?

_____
_____
_____
_____
_____
_____

What is my intention for the day?

_____
_____
_____
_____
_____
_____

What are my affirmations for the day?

_____
_____
_____
_____
_____
_____
_____

An experience I transformed to serve me through a change in perception

Daily Reflections

Date:_____

What Am I grateful for?

_____
_____
_____
_____
_____
_____

What is my intention for the day?

_____
_____
_____
_____
_____
_____

What are my affirmations for the day?

_____
_____
_____
_____
_____
_____
_____

An experience I transformed to serve me through a change in perception

_____
_____
_____
_____
_____
_____
_____

Daily Reflections

_____
_____
_____
_____
_____
_____
_____
_____
_____
_____
_____
_____
_____
_____
_____

Date:_____

What Am I grateful for?

_____
_____
_____
_____
_____
_____

What is my intention for the day?

_____
_____
_____
_____
_____
_____

What are my affirmations for the day?

_____
_____
_____
_____
_____
_____
_____

An experience I transformed to serve me through a change in perception

Daily Reflections

Date:_____

What Am I grateful for?

_____
_____
_____
_____
_____
_____

What is my intention for the day?

_____
_____
_____
_____
_____
_____

What are my affirmations for the day?

_____
_____
_____
_____
_____
_____
_____

An experience I transformed to serve me through a change in perception

Daily Reflections

Date:_____

What Am I grateful for?

_____
_____
_____
_____
_____
_____

What is my intention for the day?

_____
_____
_____
_____
_____
_____

What are my affirmations for the day?

_____
_____
_____
_____
_____
_____

An experience I transformed to serve me through a change in perception

___

Daily Reflections

Date:_____

What Am I grateful for?

_____
_____
_____
_____
_____
_____

What is my intention for the day?

_____
_____
_____
_____
_____
_____

What are my affirmations for the day?

_____
_____
_____
_____
_____
_____
_____

An experience I transformed to serve me through a change in perception
___

Daily Reflections

Date:_____

What Am I grateful for?

_____
_____
_____
_____
_____
_____

What is my intention for the day?

_____
_____
_____
_____
_____
_____

What are my affirmations for the day?

_____
_____
_____
_____
_____
_____
_____

An experience I transformed to serve me through a change in perception

Daily Reflections

Date:_____

What Am I grateful for?

_____
_____
_____
_____
_____
_____

What is my intention for the day?

_____
_____
_____
_____
_____
_____

What are my affirmations for the day?

_____
_____
_____
_____
_____
_____

An experience I transformed to serve me through a change in perception
___
___
___
___
___
___
___

Daily Reflections

___
___
___
___
___
___
___
___
___
___
___
___
___
___
___
___
___

Date:_____

What Am I grateful for?
_____
_____
_____
_____
_____
_____
_____

What is my intention for the day?
_____
_____
_____
_____
_____
_____
_____

What are my affirmations for the day?
_____
_____
_____
_____
_____
_____
_____
_____

An experience I transformed to serve me through a change in perception
___

Daily Reflections

Date:_____

What Am I grateful for?

_____
_____
_____
_____
_____
_____

What is my intention for the day?

_____
_____
_____
_____
_____
_____

What are my affirmations for the day?

_____
_____
_____
_____
_____
_____
_____

An experience I transformed to serve me through a change in perception
_____
_____
_____
_____
_____
_____
_____

Daily Reflections
_____
_____
_____
_____
_____
_____
_____
_____
_____
_____
_____
_____
_____
_____
_____
_____

Date:_____

What Am I grateful for?

_____
_____
_____
_____
_____
_____

What is my intention for the day?

_____
_____
_____
_____
_____
_____

What are my affirmations for the day?

_____
_____
_____
_____
_____
_____
_____

An experience I transformed to serve me through a change in perception

Daily Reflections

Date:_____

What Am I grateful for?

_____
_____
_____
_____
_____
_____

What is my intention for the day?

_____
_____
_____
_____
_____
_____

What are my affirmations for the day?

_____
_____
_____
_____
_____
_____
_____

An experience I transformed to serve me through a change in perception
_____
_____
_____
_____
_____
_____
_____

Daily Reflections

_____
_____
_____
_____
_____
_____
_____
_____
_____
_____
_____
_____
_____
_____
_____
_____

Date:_____

What Am I grateful for?

_____
_____
_____
_____
_____
_____

What is my intention for the day?

_____
_____
_____
_____
_____
_____

What are my affirmations for the day?

_____
_____
_____
_____
_____
_____
_____

An experience I transformed to serve me through a change in perception

Daily Reflections

Date:_____

What Am I grateful for?

_____
_____
_____
_____
_____
_____

What is my intention for the day?

_____
_____
_____
_____
_____
_____

What are my affirmations for the day?

_____
_____
_____
_____
_____
_____
_____
_____

An experience I transformed to serve me through a change in perception

___

Daily Reflections

___

Date:_____

What Am I grateful for?

_____
_____
_____
_____
_____
_____

What is my intention for the day?

_____
_____
_____
_____
_____
_____

What are my affirmations for the day?

_____
_____
_____
_____
_____
_____
_____

An experience I transformed to serve me through a change in perception

Daily Reflections

Date:_____

What Am I grateful for?

_____
_____
_____
_____
_____
_____

What is my intention for the day?

_____
_____
_____
_____
_____
_____

What are my affirmations for the day?

_____
_____
_____
_____
_____
_____
_____

An experience I transformed to serve me through a change in perception
_____
_____
_____
_____
_____
_____
_____
_____

Daily Reflections
_____
_____
_____
_____
_____
_____
_____
_____
_____
_____
_____
_____
_____
_____
_____
_____

Date:_____

What Am I grateful for?

_____
_____
_____
_____
_____
_____

What is my intention for the day?

_____
_____
_____
_____
_____
_____

What are my affirmations for the day?

_____
_____
_____
_____
_____
_____
_____

An experience I transformed to serve me through a change in perception
_____
_____
_____
_____
_____
_____

Daily Reflections
_____
_____
_____
_____
_____
_____
_____
_____
_____
_____
_____
_____
_____

Date:_____

What Am I grateful for?
_____
_____
_____
_____
_____
_____

What is my intention for the day?
_____
_____
_____
_____
_____
_____

What are my affirmations for the day?
_____
_____
_____
_____
_____
_____
_____

An experience I transformed to serve me through a change in perception

Daily Reflections

Date:_____

What Am I grateful for?

_____
_____
_____
_____
_____
_____

What is my intention for the day?

_____
_____
_____
_____
_____
_____

What are my affirmations for the day?

_____
_____
_____
_____
_____
_____
_____

An experience I transformed to serve me through a change in perception
_____
_____
_____
_____
_____
_____
_____

Daily Reflections

_____
_____
_____
_____
_____
_____
_____
_____
_____
_____
_____
_____
_____
_____
_____

Date:_____

What Am I grateful for?
_____
_____
_____
_____
_____
_____

What is my intention for the day?
_____
_____
_____
_____
_____
_____

What are my affirmations for the day?
_____
_____
_____
_____
_____
_____
_____

An experience I transformed to serve me through a change in perception
_____
_____
_____
_____
_____
_____

Daily Reflections
_____
_____
_____
_____
_____
_____
_____
_____
_____
_____
_____
_____
_____
_____

Date:_____

What Am I grateful for?
_____
_____
_____
_____
_____
_____

What is my intention for the day?
_____
_____
_____
_____
_____
_____

What are my affirmations for the day?
_____
_____
_____
_____
_____
_____
_____

An experience I transformed to serve me through a change in perception
___
___
___
___
___
___
___

Daily Reflections
___
___
___
___
___
___
___
___
___
___
___
___
___
___
___
___

Date:_____

What Am I grateful for?

_____
_____
_____
_____
_____
_____

What is my intention for the day?

_____
_____
_____
_____
_____
_____

What are my affirmations for the day?

_____
_____
_____
_____
_____
_____
_____

An experience I transformed to serve me through a change in perception

Daily Reflections

Date:_____

What Am I grateful for?

_____
_____
_____
_____
_____
_____

What is my intention for the day?

_____
_____
_____
_____
_____
_____

What are my affirmations for the day?

_____
_____
_____
_____
_____
_____
_____

An experience I transformed to serve me through a change in perception

___

Daily Reflections

___

Date:_____

What Am I grateful for?
_____
_____
_____
_____
_____
_____

What is my intention for the day?
_____
_____
_____
_____
_____
_____

What are my affirmations for the day?
_____
_____
_____
_____
_____
_____
_____

An experience I transformed to serve me through a change in perception

___

Daily Reflections

___

Date:_____

What Am I grateful for?

_____
_____
_____
_____
_____
_____

What is my intention for the day?

_____
_____
_____
_____
_____
_____

What are my affirmations for the day?

_____
_____
_____
_____
_____
_____
_____

An experience I transformed to serve me through a change in perception

_____
_____
_____
_____
_____
_____
_____

Daily Reflections

_____
_____
_____
_____
_____
_____
_____
_____
_____
_____
_____
_____
_____
_____
_____
_____
_____

Date:_____

What Am I grateful for?

_____
_____
_____
_____
_____
_____

What is my intention for the day?

_____
_____
_____
_____
_____
_____

What are my affirmations for the day?

_____
_____
_____
_____
_____
_____
_____

An experience I transformed to serve me through a change in perception

Daily Reflections

Date:_____

What Am I grateful for?
_____
_____
_____
_____
_____
_____
_____

What is my intention for the day?
_____
_____
_____
_____
_____
_____
_____

What are my affirmations for the day?
_____
_____
_____
_____
_____
_____
_____

An experience I transformed to serve me through a change in perception

_____
_____
_____
_____
_____
_____

Daily Reflections

_____
_____
_____
_____
_____
_____
_____
_____
_____
_____
_____
_____
_____
_____
_____
_____

Date:_____

What Am I grateful for?

_____
_____
_____
_____
_____
_____

What is my intention for the day?

_____
_____
_____
_____
_____
_____

What are my affirmations for the day?

_____
_____
_____
_____
_____
_____
_____

An experience I transformed to serve me through a change in perception

_____
_____
_____
_____
_____
_____

Daily Reflections

_____
_____
_____
_____
_____
_____
_____
_____
_____
_____
_____
_____
_____
_____
_____

Date:_____

What Am I grateful for?

_____
_____
_____
_____
_____
_____

What is my intention for the day?

_____
_____
_____
_____
_____
_____

What are my affirmations for the day?

_____
_____
_____
_____
_____
_____
_____

An experience I transformed to serve me through a change in perception
_____
_____
_____
_____
_____
_____
_____

Daily Reflections

_____
_____
_____
_____
_____
_____
_____
_____
_____
_____
_____
_____
_____
_____

Date:_____

What Am I grateful for?
_____
_____
_____
_____
_____
_____

What is my intention for the day?
_____
_____
_____
_____
_____
_____

What are my affirmations for the day?
_____
_____
_____
_____
_____
_____
_____

An experience I transformed to serve me through a change in perception

_____

_____

_____

_____

_____

_____

_____

Daily Reflections

_____

_____

_____

_____

_____

_____

_____

_____

_____

_____

_____

_____

_____

_____

_____

_____

Date:_____

What Am I grateful for?
_____
_____
_____
_____
_____
_____

What is my intention for the day?
_____
_____
_____
_____
_____
_____

What are my affirmations for the day?
_____
_____
_____
_____
_____
_____
_____

An experience I transformed to serve me through a change in perception

Daily Reflections

Date:_____

What Am I grateful for?

_____
_____
_____
_____
_____
_____

What is my intention for the day?

_____
_____
_____
_____
_____
_____

What are my affirmations for the day?

_____
_____
_____
_____
_____
_____

An experience I transformed to serve me through a change in perception

___

Daily Reflections

___

Date:_____

What Am I grateful for?

_____
_____
_____
_____
_____
_____

What is my intention for the day?

_____
_____
_____
_____
_____
_____

What are my affirmations for the day?

_____
_____
_____
_____
_____
_____
_____

An experience I transformed to serve me through a change in perception
___

Daily Reflections
___

Date:_____

What Am I grateful for?

_____
_____
_____
_____
_____
_____

What is my intention for the day?

_____
_____
_____
_____
_____
_____

What are my affirmations for the day?

_____
_____
_____
_____
_____
_____
_____

An experience I transformed to serve me through a change in perception

_____
_____
_____
_____
_____
_____
_____

Daily Reflections

_____
_____
_____
_____
_____
_____
_____
_____
_____
_____
_____
_____
_____
_____
_____
_____
_____

Date:_____

What Am I grateful for?
_____
_____
_____
_____
_____
_____

What is my intention for the day?
_____
_____
_____
_____
_____
_____

What are my affirmations for the day?
_____
_____
_____
_____
_____
_____
_____

An experience I transformed to serve me through a change in perception
_____
_____
_____
_____
_____
_____

Daily Reflections

_____
_____
_____
_____
_____
_____
_____
_____
_____
_____
_____
_____
_____
_____

Date:_____

What Am I grateful for?

_____
_____
_____
_____
_____
_____

What is my intention for the day?

_____
_____
_____
_____
_____
_____

What are my affirmations for the day?

_____
_____
_____
_____
_____
_____
_____

An experience I transformed to serve me through a change in perception

_____
_____
_____
_____
_____
_____

Daily Reflections

_____
_____
_____
_____
_____
_____
_____
_____
_____
_____
_____
_____
_____
_____
_____

Date:_____

What Am I grateful for?
_____
_____
_____
_____
_____
_____

What is my intention for the day?
_____
_____
_____
_____
_____
_____

What are my affirmations for the day?
_____
_____
_____
_____
_____
_____
_____

An experience I transformed to serve me through a change in perception

Daily Reflections

Date:_____

What Am I grateful for?

_____
_____
_____
_____
_____
_____

What is my intention for the day?

_____
_____
_____
_____
_____
_____

What are my affirmations for the day?

_____
_____
_____
_____
_____
_____
_____

An experience I transformed to serve me through a change in perception

Daily Reflections

Date:_____

What Am I grateful for?
_____
_____
_____
_____
_____
_____
_____

What is my intention for the day?
_____
_____
_____
_____
_____
_____
_____

What are my affirmations for the day?
_____
_____
_____
_____
_____
_____
_____
_____

An experience I transformed to serve me through a change in perception

Daily Reflections

Date:_____

What Am I grateful for?
_____
_____
_____
_____
_____
_____

What is my intention for the day?
_____
_____
_____
_____
_____
_____

What are my affirmations for the day?
_____
_____
_____
_____
_____
_____
_____

An experience I transformed to serve me through a change in perception
___

Daily Reflections
___

Date:_____

What Am I grateful for?
_____
_____
_____
_____
_____

What is my intention for the day?
_____
_____
_____
_____
_____

What are my affirmations for the day?
_____
_____
_____
_____
_____
_____

An experience I transformed to serve me through a change in perception
___
___
___
___
___
___
___

Daily Reflections
___
___
___
___
___
___
___
___
___
___
___
___
___
___
___

Date:_____

What Am I grateful for?

_____
_____
_____
_____
_____
_____

What is my intention for the day?

_____
_____
_____
_____
_____
_____

What are my affirmations for the day?

_____
_____
_____
_____
_____
_____
_____

An experience I transformed to serve me through a change in perception

Daily Reflections

Date:_____

What Am I grateful for?

_____
_____
_____
_____
_____
_____

What is my intention for the day?

_____
_____
_____
_____
_____
_____

What are my affirmations for the day?

_____
_____
_____
_____
_____
_____
_____

An experience I transformed to serve me through a change in perception

_____
_____
_____
_____
_____
_____

Daily Reflections

_____
_____
_____
_____
_____
_____
_____
_____
_____
_____
_____
_____
_____
_____
_____

Date:_____

What Am I grateful for?

_____
_____
_____
_____
_____
_____

What is my intention for the day?

_____
_____
_____
_____
_____
_____

What are my affirmations for the day?

_____
_____
_____
_____
_____
_____
_____

An experience I transformed to serve me through a change in perception
___
___
___
___
___
___
___

Daily Reflections

___
___
___
___
___
___
___
___
___
___
___
___
___
___
___
___

Date:_____

What Am I grateful for?

_____
_____
_____
_____
_____
_____

What is my intention for the day?

_____
_____
_____
_____
_____
_____

What are my affirmations for the day?

_____
_____
_____
_____
_____
_____
_____

An experience I transformed to serve me through a change in perception
___

Daily Reflections
___

Date:_____

What Am I grateful for?

_____
_____
_____
_____
_____
_____

What is my intention for the day?

_____
_____
_____
_____
_____
_____

What are my affirmations for the day?

_____
_____
_____
_____
_____
_____
_____

An experience I transformed to serve me through a change in perception
___

Daily Reflections

Date:_____

What Am I grateful for?

_____
_____
_____
_____
_____
_____

What is my intention for the day?

_____
_____
_____
_____
_____
_____

What are my affirmations for the day?

_____
_____
_____
_____
_____
_____
_____

An experience I transformed to serve me through a change in perception

Daily Reflections

Date:_____

What Am I grateful for?
_____
_____
_____
_____
_____
_____

What is my intention for the day?
_____
_____
_____
_____
_____
_____

What are my affirmations for the day?
_____
_____
_____
_____
_____
_____
_____

An experience I transformed to serve me through a change in perception

Daily Reflections

Date:_____

What Am I grateful for?

_____
_____
_____
_____
_____
_____

What is my intention for the day?

_____
_____
_____
_____
_____
_____

What are my affirmations for the day?

_____
_____
_____
_____
_____
_____
_____

An experience I transformed to serve me through a change in perception
_____
_____
_____
_____
_____
_____
_____

Daily Reflections

_____
_____
_____
_____
_____
_____
_____
_____
_____
_____
_____
_____
_____
_____
_____

Date:_____

What Am I grateful for?

_____
_____
_____
_____
_____

What is my intention for the day?

_____
_____
_____
_____
_____

What are my affirmations for the day?

_____
_____
_____
_____
_____

An experience I transformed to serve me through a change in perception

Daily Reflections

Date:_____

What Am I grateful for?
_____
_____
_____
_____
_____
_____

What is my intention for the day?
_____
_____
_____
_____
_____
_____

What are my affirmations for the day?
_____
_____
_____
_____
_____
_____
_____

An experience I transformed to serve me through a change in perception

Daily Reflections

Date:_____

What Am I grateful for?
_____
_____
_____
_____
_____
_____

What is my intention for the day?
_____
_____
_____
_____
_____
_____

What are my affirmations for the day?
_____
_____
_____
_____
_____
_____
_____

An experience I transformed to serve me through a change in perception
___
___
___
___
___
___
___

Daily Reflections
___
___
___
___
___
___
___
___
___
___
___
___
___
___
___
___

Date:_____

What Am I grateful for?

_____
_____
_____
_____
_____
_____

What is my intention for the day?

_____
_____
_____
_____
_____
_____

What are my affirmations for the day?

_____
_____
_____
_____
_____
_____
_____

An experience I transformed to serve me through a change in perception

Daily Reflections

Date:_____

What Am I grateful for?

_____
_____
_____
_____
_____
_____

What is my intention for the day?

_____
_____
_____
_____
_____
_____

What are my affirmations for the day?

_____
_____
_____
_____
_____
_____
_____

An experience I transformed to serve me through a change in perception
_____
_____
_____
_____
_____
_____
_____

Daily Reflections
_____
_____
_____
_____
_____
_____
_____
_____
_____
_____
_____
_____
_____
_____
_____

Date:_____

What Am I grateful for?

_____
_____
_____
_____
_____
_____

What is my intention for the day?

_____
_____
_____
_____
_____
_____

What are my affirmations for the day?

_____
_____
_____
_____
_____
_____
_____

An experience I transformed to serve me through a change in perception
___

Daily Reflections

___

Date:_____

What Am I grateful for?

_____
_____
_____
_____
_____
_____

What is my intention for the day?

_____
_____
_____
_____
_____
_____

What are my affirmations for the day?

_____
_____
_____
_____
_____
_____
_____

An experience I transformed to serve me through a change in perception

_____
_____
_____
_____
_____
_____

Daily Reflections

_____
_____
_____
_____
_____
_____
_____
_____
_____
_____
_____
_____
_____
_____

www.ingramcontent.com/pod-product-compliance
Lightning Source LLC
Chambersburg PA
CBHW041324110526
44592CB00021B/2809